CONCERNING
THE INNER LIFE

CONCERNING THE INNER LIFE

Evelyn Underhill

ONEWORLD

OXFORD

CONCERNING THE INNER LIFE

Oneworld Publications
(Sales and Editorial)
185 Banbury Road
Oxford OX2 7AR
England
http://www.oneworld-publications.com

Oneworld Publications
(US Marketing Office)
160 N. Washington St.
4th Floor, Boston
MA 02114
USA

First published by Oneworld Publications 1995
This edition © Oneworld Publications 1999
Reprinted 2000

ISBN 1–85168–194–9

Cover design by Design Deluxe
Printed in England by Clays Ltd, St Ives plc

CONTENTS

PREFACE

THE THREE ADDRESSES CONTAINED IN THIS LITTLE BOOK were delivered at a school for clergy in the North of England; and are now published at the request of some of those who heard them. A few additions have been made, especially to the second of the series; but their original character – that of intimate and informal talks rather than lectures – has been retained.

Some of the problems of the spiritual life are here considered with special reference to the needs, difficulties and duties of the busy parish priest. But since in essence many of these problems are the same for all whose religious interests have passed from the sphere of notion to the sphere of experience, I hope that others may find here something relevant to their own situation; and will extend to this amateur effort the generous sympathy and tolerance with which my clerical hearers first received it.

E. U. , 1926

In Whom we know and see all things,
and by Whom we learn ever to simplify and
unify our multiplicities and occupations,
and our outward actions; by looking beyond
and through all our works, however great
and divine they may appear.

GERLAC PETERSEN

Part I

❂

THE HEART OF
PERSONAL RELIGION

WE ARE TO CONSIDER IN THE COURSE OF THESE addresses some of the problems most intimately concerning that which is generally known as the 'inner life'; and this in their special relation to the needs of the parish priest and religious teacher. And by the term 'inner life' we shall here mean all that conditions the relation of the individual soul with God; the deepening and expansion of the spiritual sense; in fact, the heart of personal religion. I feel a great diffidence in coming before you, as an ordinary laywoman, to speak of such matters as these; since they are, after all, your peculiar and professional concern. Indeed, I only presume to do so because I care about these things very much, and have some leisure to think about them; and so venture to put at your service certain conclusions to which I have come. If many of these are already familiar to you, as they probably are, you must forgive me.

We start from the obvious fact, that as persons professionally concerned to teach and demonstrate the truths of religion, to spread the knowledge of God, and to work with souls, the problems of the personal spiritual life are of the most transcendent importance to you: indeed, that they concern you more certainly and directly than they do Christians of any other type. The very first requisite for a minister of religion is that his own inner life should be maintained in a healthy state; his own contact with God be steady and true. But just because you are ministers of religion, and therefore committed to perpetual external activities, this fostering and feeding of the inner life is often in some ways far more difficult for you, than it is for those for whom you work and whom you teach. The time which you have at your disposal for the purpose is limited; and the rest of your time is more or less fully occupied with external religious and philanthropic activities, often of a most exacting kind. There is a constant drain on your spiritual resources, which you simply must make good: while the relief and change so necessary for all of us if our spiritual lives are to remain keen, vivid, real, is often lacking in your case, going incessantly as you do and must from one form of religious activity to another.

This being so, it does become immensely important, doesn't it, for you to have a clear view of your own spiritual position and needs, a clear idea of the essentials of your situation; and to plot out the time which you have at your own disposal as well as you possibly can? The clergy above all others need to learn, and raise to the level of habit, George Fox's art of 'seeing all things in the Universal Light'. Yet it very often happens that busy and driven parish priests entirely lose sight not merely of their own spiritual position, but also of this great spiritual landscape in which they are placed; by concentrating all the while on those details of it that specially concern them. They cannot see the forest, because they are attending so faithfully to the trees. It is surely a first charge on their devotional lives, to recover that sense of the forest, which gives all their meaning to the trees.

For this purpose, it seems to me, neither a hard and fast liturgic scheme, nor the most carefully planned theological reading, nor any sort of dreamy devotionalism, is going to be of use to you. The primary thing, I believe, that will be of use is a conception, as clear and rich and deep as you are able to get it, first of the Splendour of God; and next of your own souls over against that Splendour of God; and last of the sort of interior life which your election of His service demands. God – the soul – its election of Him – the three fundamental realities of religion. If these realities do not rule the mind and heart of the priest, how is it conceivable that he can do the work of God in the souls of others?

I said: 'the sort of interior life which your election demands'. Because that will be, or should be, distinct in kind from the inner life of the average Christian. The soul of a priest – in fact, the soul of every religious worker – stands in a special relation towards God and other souls. He has spiritual problems which are special to himself. He is one of the assistant shepherds, not one of the sheep. He has got to stick it out in all weathers; to be always ready, always serving, always eager to feed and save. An unremitting, patient, fostering care, the willing endurance of exhaustion, hardship, and risk: all these things may be asked of him. He is constantly called upon to give out spiritual energy and sympathy. And he has got to maintain his own supplies, his own religious health and suppleness, in a manner adequate to that demand; so to deepen his own life, that he is capable of deepening the lives of others. In the striking phrase of St Bernard, if he is adequately to fulfil all his obligations, he must be a reservoir and not a canal.

Now there is only one way in which it is possible for the religious teacher to do all this; and that is by enriching his sense of God. And that enrichment of the sense of God is surely the crying need of our current Christianity. A shallow religiousness, the tendency to be content with a bright ethical piety wrongly called practical Christianity, a nice, brightly varnished this-world faith, seems to me to be one of the ruling defects of institutional religion at the present time. We are drifting towards a religion which consciously or unconsciously keeps its eye on humanity rather than on Deity – which lays all the stress on service, and hardly any of the stress on awe: and that is a type of religion which in practice does not wear well. It does little for the soul in those awful moments when the pain and mystery of life are most deeply felt. It does not provide a place for that profound experience which Tauler called 'suffering in God'. It does not lead to sanctity: and sanctity after all is the religious goal. It does not fit those who accept it as adequate for the solemn privilege of guiding souls to God – and is not guiding souls to God the object of the pastoral life? In fact, it turns its back on the most profound gifts made by Christianity to the human race. I do not think we can deny that there is at present a definite trend in the direction of religion of this shallow social type; and it will only be checked if and in so far as the clergy are themselves real men of prayer, learning to know at first hand more and more deeply – and so more and more humbly – the ineffable realities to which they have given their lives. Therefore to become and to continue to be a real man of prayer, seems to me the first duty of a parish priest.

What then are real people of prayer? They are those who deliberately will and steadily desire that their intercourse with God and other souls shall be controlled and actuated at every point by God Himself; those who have so far developed and educated their spiritual sense, that their supernatural environment is more real and solid to them than their natural environment. Men and women of prayer are not necessarily those who say a number of offices, or abound in detailed intercessions, but they are children of God, who are and know themselves to be in the depths of their souls attached to God, and are wholly and entirely guided by the Creative Spirit in their prayer and their work. This is not merely a bit of pious language. It is a description, as real and concrete as I can make it, of the only really apostolic life. Every Christian starts with a chance of it; but only a few develop it. The laity distinguish in a moment the clergy who have it from the clergy who have it not: there is nothing that you can do for God or for the souls of men, which exceeds in importance the achievement of that spiritual temper and attitude.

Consider. As Christians we are committed, are we not, to a belief in the priority of the supernatural world;

the actual presence, and working within visible appearance, of the Creative Spirit of God? For the parishes to which you are sent you are, or should be, the main links with that supernatural world; the main channels of God's action on souls. You are those in whom the hope of a more intense spiritual life for those parishes is centred: those in whom for this purpose God has placed His trust. An abasing thought, isn't it? Even individuals among the laity who are used in such a way as that find it an overwhelming experience; and this gives some clue to the profound humility and sense of awe which their vocation must produce in priests; the constant and delicate susceptibility to the pressure of the Spirit which is required by their work.

There you are, moving through life: immersed in the world of succession and change, constantly claimed by the little serial duties and interests of your career, and yet ringed round by the solemn horizon of eternity, informed by its invisible powers. And – because you are priests – even more than is the case with other men, all that you do, feel and think as you move through this changing life, is going to affect all the other souls whom you touch, and condition their relation with that unchanging Real. Through you, they may be attracted to or repelled by the spiritual life. You are held tight in that double relationship; to those other changing souls and to that changeless God. What you are like, and what your relation to God is like, must and will affect all those whom you visit, preach to, pray with, and to whom you give the sacraments. It will make the difference between Church services which are spiritual experiences to those attending them, and Church services which consist in the formal recitation of familiar words. We, the laity, know instantly the difference between the churches which are served with love and devotion and those which are not. And we know from this what their ministers are like. And what you are like is going to depend on your secret life of prayer; on the steady orientation of your souls to the Reality of God. Called upon to practise in their fullness the two great commandments, you can only hope to get the second one right if you are completely controlled by the first. And that will depend on the quality of your secret inner life.

Now by the quality of our inner lives I do not mean something characterized by ferocious intensity and strain. I mean, rather, such a humble and genial devotedness as we find in the most loving of the saints. I mean the quality which makes contagious Christians; makes people *catch* the love of God from you. Because they ought not to be able to help doing this, if you have really got it: if you yourselves feel the love, joy and peace, the utter delightfulness of the consecrated life –

and this to such an extent, that every formal act of worship in church is filled with the free spontaneous worship of your soul. That is what wins people above all. It raises the simplest vocal prayer, the most commonplace of hymns, the most elaborate ceremonial action to the same level of supernatural truth. People want to see and feel this in those who come to them with the credentials of religion: the joy, the delightfulness, the transfiguration of hard dull work and of suffering, which irradiate the real Christian life. You can't do more for anybody than give them that, can you? For that means real redemption here and now; the healing of all our psychic conflicts, all our worries and resistances and sense of injustice.

You are sent to a world full of tortured, twisted, overdriven souls: and sometimes nowadays you are told, that in order to help them better, you ought to study psychology – by which is usually meant morbid psychology. I do not deny that this may be very useful knowledge for the clergy, and save them from many disastrous mistakes. But all the same, I think it would be much more practical, more use to your people in the end, to spend that time and strength in deepening and increasing your own love of God: for it is only through adoration and attention that we make our personal discoveries about Him. How are you going to show these souls, who need it so dreadfully, the joy and delightfulness of God and surrender to God, unless you have it yourselves? But that means giving time, patience, effort to such a special discipline and cultivation of your attention as artists must give, if they are to enter deeply into the reality and joy of natural loveliness and impart it in their work. Do you see the great facts and splendours of religion with the eye of an artist and a lover, or with the eye of a businessman or -woman, or the eye of the man in the street? Is your sense of wonder and mystery keen and deep? Such a sense of wonder and mystery, such a living delight in God, is, of course, in technical language a grace. It is something added, given, to the natural part of us. But, like all other graces, its reception by us depends very largely on the exercise of our will and our desire, on our mental and emotional openness and plasticity. It will not be forced upon us. And we show our will and desire, keep ourselves plastic, in and through the character of our prayer. You remember Jeremy Taylor's saying: 'Prayer is only the body of the bird – desires are its wings.'

All this means that the secret prayer of the priest must have a certain contemplative colour about it: that one of its main functions must be to feed and expand his sense and desire of God. We will consider later some of the ways in which he may best achieve this.

Now, let us only get this supernatural orientation firmly fixed in our minds, as the central character of a fruitful inner life. The English mystic, Walter Hilton, said that the City of Jerusalem, the city of the love of God, was built 'by the perfection of a man's work, and a little touch of contemplation'. And by contemplative prayer, I do not mean any abnormal sort of activity or experience, still less a deliberate and artificial passivity. I just mean the sort of prayer that aims at God in and for Himself and not for any of His gifts whatever, and more and more profoundly rests in Him alone: what St Paul, that vivid realist, meant by being *rooted* and *grounded*. When I read those words, I always think of a forest tree. First of the bright and changeful tuft that shows itself to the world, and produces the immense spread of boughs and branches, the succession and abundance of leaves and fruits. Then of the vast unseen system of roots, perhaps greater than the branches in strength and extent, with their tenacious attachments, their fan-like system of delicate filaments and their power of silently absorbing food. On that profound and secret life the whole growth and stability of the tree depend. It is rooted and grounded in a hidden world.

That was the image in Paul's mind, I suppose, when he talked of this as the one prayer he made for his converts and fellow workers; and said that he desired it

Ephesians 2 1

for them so that they could 'be able to comprehend what is the breadth and length and depth and height' – a splendour of realization unachieved by theology – and be 'filled with all the fullness of God': in other words, draw their spiritual energy direct from its supernatural source. You know that St Bernard called this the 'business of all businesses'; because it controls all the rest, and gives meaning to all the rest – perpetually renews our contact with reality. Ought not our devotional life to be such as to frame in us the habit of such recourse to God as the Ground of the soul? Should it not educate our whole mental machinery, feeling, imagination, will and thought, for this?

St Ignatius Loyola based the whole of his great Spiritual Exercises on one fundamental truth: 'Man was created for this end – to praise, reverence and serve the Lord his God.' This sounds all right, indeed almost obvious, when one says it. It slips by, like so many religious phrases, almost unchecked. But if we stop and look at it, and especially at the chosen order of the terms which that great saint and psychologist employed, what does it mean? It means that one's first duty is adoration; and one's second duty is awe; and only one's third duty is service. And that for those three things and nothing else, addressed to God and no one else, you and I and all the other countless human creatures evolved upon the surface of this planet were created.

We observe then, that two of the three things for which our souls were made are matters of attitude, of relation: adoration and awe. Unless those two are right, the last of the triad, service, won't be right. Unless the whole of your priestly life is a movement of praise and adoration, unless it is instinct with awe, the work which that life produces won't be much good. And if that is true, it follows that the Christian revelation, the work done by Christ in men's souls, has also as its main object the promotion of God's glory, the shining out of His Reality more and more fully through our acts: the increase of our wide-open, loving, selfless adoration, the deepening of our creaturely awe, the expanding of our consecration in service. And all this must happen in you, before you can give it to your people, mustn't it? You have to show them in your own person the literal truth of the other great Ignatian saying: 'I come from God – I belong to God – I am destined for God!'

This, then, seems the first consideration which should be before the mind of the priest, in planning a personal devotional life. It means that attention to God must be your primary religious activity, and this for the strictly practical reason that without that attention to God, all other religious activities will lose their worth, that the life of the minister of religion depends almost entirely for its value on the extent to which it is bathed in the Divine Light. This is the first term of all religious life and thought; and probably the term to which most modern Christians give least undivided attention.

Yet how necessary it is, isn't it, for you, kept perpetually on the move, incessantly distracted by the countless details of parochial life, and exposed too to the dangers of monotony and spiritual deadness that lurk in the perpetual recitation of set forms, to form early and to feed regularly the habit of recourse to the changeless Eternity which supports that life? It is the ultimate object of all those devoted, ceaseless and changeful activities of yours, to bring into the lives of those for and with whom you work something of that changeless temper of Eternity. If you, with your special facilities and training, do not manage to do this, it is not particularly likely that anyone else will do it and your power of doing it depends upon your possession of it. There is a beautiful prayer which is often said at the end of the Office of Compline asking that those who are wearied by this changeful world may repose on the Eternal Changelessness. Are these mere words to us, or do they represent a vivid fact? We can almost test the healthiness of our own inner lives by the answer we give to that question. The writings of the saints and of many lesser lovers of God prove to us again and again that the sense of the Eternal as a vivid fact can become so integrated with the life of the soul, that it can reach the level of habit. In you at least it has got to reach that level of habit, if you are completely to fulfil your vocation; because that vocation consists, when we get down to fundamentals, in bringing the eternal realities of God to the souls of men, and thus participating in the continued redemptive action of Spirit on the world.

A priest is or should be an agent of the supernatural. We ordinary people hustle along; trying to get through the detailed work of each day, and respond reasonably well to its demands, opportunities and obligations. We are obsessed by the ceaseless chain of events, and forget for the most part the mystery that surrounds us; the overplus of spiritual reality and power, far beyond anything that we are able to conceive, and yet constantly and intimately conditioning us. But you cannot afford to do that. Your supernatural status matters supremely to every soul that is in your charge, and will be the main factor in bringing other souls into your charge. And one of the chief things that will help you to develop a sense of that supernatural status, will be to keep steadily in view the great central truths of religion; training yourselves to their realization and forming the habit of constant recourse to their healing and purifying influences.

The beginning, then, of a strong and fruitful inner life in the clergyman or religious worker seems to me to depend on the thorough realization of these facts. It requires, not merely the acceptance but the full first-hand apprehension, of the ruling truth of the richly living spaceless and unchanging God; blazing in the spiritual sky, yet intimately present within the world of events, moulding and conditioning every phase of life. The religion of the priest, if it is to give power and convey certitude, must be from first to last a theocentric religion; and it must be fed by a devotional practice based upon that objective Power and Presence, and neither on your own subjective feelings, cravings, and needs, nor on the feelings, cravings, and needs of those among whom you work. Once you have made that utter independence and given-ness of God your point of departure, your whole conception of life will be affected; and many little fusses about the details of that life, caused by the extraordinary degree of importance we attach to our mere active service, will vanish away.

I feel more and more convinced that only a spirituality which thus puts the whole emphasis on the Reality of God, perpetually turning to Him, losing itself in Him, refusing to allow even the most pressing work or practical problems, even sin and failure, to distract from God – only this is a safe foundation for spiritual work. This alone is able to keep alive the awed, adoring sense of the mysteries among which we move, and of the tiny bit which at the best we ourselves can apprehend of them – and yet, considering that immensity and our tininess, the marvel of what we do know and feel.

A great woman of the last century, Mother Janet Stuart, was accustomed to say to her novices: 'Think glorious thoughts of God – and serve Him with a quiet mind!' And it is surely a fact that the more glorious and more spacious our thoughts of Him are, the greater the quietude and confidence with which we do our detailed work will be. Not controversial thoughts, or dry academic thoughts, or anxious worried thoughts, or narrow conventional thoughts. All these bring contraction instead of expansion to our souls; and we all know that this inner sense of contraction or expansion is an unfailing test of our spiritual state. But awed and delighted thoughts of a Reality and Holiness that is inconceivable to us, and yet that is Love. A Reality that pours itself out in and through the simplest forms and accidents, and makes itself known under the homeliest symbols; that is completely present in and with us, determining us at every moment of our lives. Such meditations as these keep our windows open towards Eternity; and preserve us from that insidious pious stuffiness which is the moth and rust of the dedicated life.

The inner life means an ever-deepening awareness of all this: the slowly growing and concrete realization of a Life and a Spirit within us immeasurably exceeding our own, and absorbing, transmuting, supernaturalizing our lives by all ways and at all times. It means the loving sense of God, as so immeasurably beyond us as to keep us in a constant attitude of humblest awe – and yet so deeply and closely with us, as to invite our clinging trust and loyal love. This, it seems to me, is what theological terms such as transcendence and immanence can come to mean to us when reinterpreted in the life of prayer.

Surely such a personal reinterpretation is a deeply important part of your pastoral work; a part of the apostolic process of sanctifying yourselves for the sake of other souls, of making yourselves fit to attract and win other souls. For you will only bring men and women to the love of God in so far as you yourselves have got it; and can only help them to make sense of that world of time and events which so greatly bewilders them, in so far as you are able to bring into it the spirit of Eternity. That is what you are for. That is the spiritual food which you are charged to give to the sheep. It is that love of God and that peace and presence of Eternity for which souls are now so hungry; and your power of really feeding them depends absolutely on your own secret life towards God.

Again, the world is full of jangling noises. You know that there are better melodies. But you will never transmit the heavenly music to others unless you yourselves are tuned in to it: and that, once more, means giving to it careful and undivided attention during part of each day. Do you feel sure, as you move about among your people, as you take services, administer sacraments, preach, and so forth, that you bring with you and impart to them an absolute spiritual certitude? Because if you are not doing that, you are not really doing your job, are you?

Now if you are to convey that spiritual certitude, it is plain that you must yourselves be spiritually alive. And to be spiritually alive means to be growing and changing; not to settle down among a series of systematized beliefs and duties, but to endure and go on enduring the strains, conflicts and difficulties incident to development. 'The soul', said Baron von Hügel, 'is a Force or an Energy: and Holiness is the *growth* of that energy in love, in full Being, in creative, spiritual Personality.' One chief object of personal religion is the promoting of that growth of the soul; the wise feeding and training of it. However busy we may be, however mature and efficient we may seem, that growth, if we are real Christians, must go on. Even the greatest spiritual teachers, such as St Paul and St Augustine, could never afford to relax the tension of their own spiritual lives; they seemed never to stand still, were never afraid of conflict and change. Their souls too were growing entities, with a potential capacity for love, adoration and creative service; in other words, for holiness, the achievement of the stature of Christ. A saint is simply a human being whose soul has thus grown up to its full stature, by full and generous response to its environment, God. He has achieved a deeper, bigger life than the rest of us, a more wonderful contact with the mysteries of the Universe; a life of infinite possibility, the term of which he never feels that he has reached.

That desire and willingness for growth at all costs, that sense of great unreached possibilities which await the fully expanded human soul, is important for us all; but surely especially important for priests? It is imperative that those who are to teach religion and guide souls should steadily enlarge their conception of and capacity for God; yet how many adult Christian workers go on, as they should do, steadily expanding towards Eternity, the one thing, I suppose, which more than any other testifies to our spiritual vitality? If we do not grow thus, the origin of that defect is and can only be in the poverty of our own inner lives of prayer and mortification, keeping that spiritual vitality at low ebb. Prayer and mortification are hard words; but after all that which they involve is simply communion with God and discipline of self. They are the names of those two fundamental and inseparable activities which temper our natural resources to our supernatural work; and every Christian worker must have in his or her life the bracing and humbling influences of such continuous self-surrender and self-conquest. They involve a ceaseless gentle discipline; but being a disciple means living a disciplined life, and it is not very likely that you will get other disciples, unless you are one first.

The saintly and simple Curé d'Ars was once asked the secret of his abnormal success in converting souls. He replied that it was done by being very indulgent to others and very hard on himself; a recipe which retains all its virtue still. And this power of being outwardly genial and inwardly austere, which is the real Christian temper, depends entirely on the use we make of the time set apart for personal religion. It is always achieved if courageously and faithfully sought; and there are no heights of love and holiness to which it cannot lead, no limits to the power which it can exercise over the souls of men and women.

We have the saints to show us that these things are actually possible: that one human soul can rescue and transfigure another, and can endure for it redemptive hardship and pain. We may allow that the saints are specialists; but they are specialists in a career to which all Christians are called. They have achieved, as it were, the classic status. They are the advance guard of the army; but we, after all, are marching in the main ranks. The whole army is dedicated to the same supernatural cause; and we ought to envisage it as a whole, and to remember that every one of us wears the same uniform as the saints, has access to the same privileges, is taught the same drill and fed with the same food. The difference between them and us is a difference in degree, not in kind. They possess, and we most conspicuously lack, a certain maturity and depth of soul caused by the perfect flowering in them of self-oblivious love, joy and peace. We recognize in them a finished product, a genuine work of God. But this power and beauty of the saints is on the human side simply the result of their faithful life of prayer; and is something to which, in various degrees, every Christian worker can attain. Therefore we ought all to be a little bit like them; to have a sort of family likeness, to share the family point of view.

If we ask of the saints how they achieved spiritual effectiveness, they are only able to reply that, in so far as they did it themselves, they did it by love and prayer. A love that is very humble and homely; a prayer that is full of adoration and of confidence. Love and prayer, on their lips, are not mere nice words; they are the names of tremendous powers, able to transform in a literal sense human personality and make it more and more that which it is meant to be – the agent of the Holy Spirit in the world. Plainly then, it is essential to give time or to get time somehow for self-training in this love and this prayer, in order to develop those powers. It is true that in their essence they are 'given', but the gift is only fully made our own by a patient and generous effort of the soul. Spiritual achievement costs much, though never as much as it is worth. It means at the very least the painful development and persevering, steady exercise of a faculty that most of us have allowed to get slack. It means an inward if not an outward asceticism: a virtual if not an actual mysticism.

People talk about mysticism as if it were something quite separate from practical religion; whereas, as a matter of fact, it is the intense heart of all practical religion, and no one without some touch of it is contagious and able to win souls. What *is* mysticism? It is in its widest sense the reaching out of the soul to contact with those eternal realities which are the subject matter of religion. And the mystical life is the complete life of love and prayer which transmutes those objects of belief into living realities: love and prayer directed to God for God Himself, and not for any gain for ourselves. Therefore there should surely be some mystical element in the inner life of every real priest.

All our external religious activities – services, communions, formal devotions, good works – these are either the expressions or the support of this inward life of loving adherence. We must have such outward expressions and supports, because we are not pure spirits but human beings, receiving through our senses the messages of Reality. But all their beauty is from within; and the degree in which we can either exhibit or apprehend that beauty depends on our own inward state. I think that if this were more fully realized, a great deal of the hostility which is now shown to institutional religion by good and earnest people would break down. It is your part, isn't it, to show them that it is true: to transmute by your love those dead forms of which they are always complaining, and make of them the chalice of the Spirit of Life?

In one of the Apocryphal Gospels of the Infancy there is a story of how the child Jesus, picking up the clay sparrows with which the other boys were playing, threw them into the air, where they became living birds. As a legend, we may regard this as an absurdity. As a spiritual parable it is profoundly true.

Part II

✪

THE GOALS OF
INNER LIFE

WE HAVE CONSIDERED IN A GENERAL SENSE THE supernatural situation of workers for God; their total and direct dependence upon spiritual resources, and the duty of self-sanctification which lies upon them, so that they may become fit agents and tools of the Spirit. We have seen that a gradual and steady growth is demanded of them: and this growth must be in two directions – in depth, and in expansive love. They are called to an ever-deepening, more awe-struck and realistic adoration of God, which shall be the true measure of their spiritual status. They are also called to an ever-widening and more generous outflow of loving interest towards their fellow human beings. It was Ruysbroeck, one of the greatest of contemplatives, who declared the result of a perfected life of prayer to be 'a wide-spreading love to all in common'. But it is only in so far as he or she succeeds in achieving the deepness, that a person can hope to win and maintain that expansiveness. We come therefore to the practical means by which this can be attained, and the practical aims which we should put before us.

There are features in the situation of the modern religious worker which are peculiar to our own times. The pace and pressure of life is now so great, the mass of detail supposed to be necessary to organized religion has so immensely increased, that it has created an entirely new situation. It is more difficult than ever before for the parish priest to obtain time and quiet of soul for the deepening of his own devotional life. Yet if it is true that the vocation of the clergy is first and foremost to the care of souls, and if only persons of prayer can hope to win and deal with souls in an adequate and fruitful way, then surely this problem of how to obtain time and peace for attention to the spiritual world, is primary for each of you. It is, indeed, a problem which everyone who takes religion seriously is obliged to face and to solve. Everyone must decide, according to his circumstances, how much time each day he can spare for this; and then further decide what in his position, and with due regard to his needs and nature, is the very best way of using that time. The amount of time which can be given and the way that it is used will vary between soul and soul; and the first snag to avoid is surely that of adopting a set scheme because we have read about it in a book, or because it suits somebody else.

We shall find, when we look into our own souls, or study those with whom we have to deal, that there is an immense variation among them; both in aptitude, and in method of approaching God. We shall discover that only certain devotional books and certain devotional symbols and practices truly have meaning for us; whilst others will appeal to other people. Some of us belong predominantly to the institutional, some to the ascetical and ethical, some to the mystical type; and within these great classes and types of spirituality, there is an infinite variety of temper and degree. The first thing we have to find out is the kind of practice that suits *our* souls – ours, not someone else's, and now, at this stage of its growth. You have to find and develop the prayer that fully employs you and yet does not overstrain you; the prayer in which you are quite supple before God; the prayer that refreshes, braces and expands you, and is best able to carry you over the inevitable fluctuations of spiritual level and mood. But in thus making up your minds to use that method towards which you are most deeply and persistently attracted, and to feed your own souls on the food that you can digest, you must nevertheless retain an entire and supple willingness to give others, if desirable, a quite different diet, encourage in them another sort of practice. More than this, you must for their sakes try to learn all you can about methods other than your own. The clergy are the very last people in the world who can afford to be devotional specialists. And the way to avoid being a devotional specialist is to keep one's eye on the great objectives of prayer; never forgetting that these great objectives belong to Eternal Life, while all forms and methods without exception belong to the world of change, and only have value as expressing and improving the communion of the soul with God.

Look now at the aim which should condition your inner life. This aim, in your case, cannot and must not be that of becoming a contemplative pure and simple. It must rather be to transfuse your whole life of action and service with the spirit of contemplation. The vocation of the Christian minister is to the mixed life of prayer and service of which the classic pattern is seen in Christ: the highest, the most difficult, the most complete human life that we know. It is a life of looking and of working, which unites the will, the imagination and the heart; concentrates them on one single aim. In the recollected hours of prayer and meditation you do the looking; in the active and expansive hours you do the working. Such a regime, faithfully followed, will slowly but surely transform the personality of those pursuing it. Therefore the time that you give to private devotion must always be thought of as contributing to this: feeding and expanding your spirit, making you more and more capable of 'being to the Eternal Goodness what his own hand is to a man' – a supple and a living tool. It must be such a period of concentrated attention as will gather the spiritual energy which afterwards overflows into your liturgic and pastoral work. It must form in you such an ever-deepening spiritual communion, as shall establish and feed in you an adherence to God, which you can carry right through the external tasks of your day: shall warm and illuminate your ministry whether of services or of teaching.

Especially, I think, these times of secret prayer should train the priest to live more and more intensely towards God in the conducting of liturgic prayer. You do far more for your congregations, for helping them to understand what prayer really is, and to practise it, for quickening their religious sensitiveness, by your un-selfconscious absorption in God during services, than you can hope to do by any amount of sermons, instructions, introduction of novel and attractive features, etc. These congregations are probably far too shy to come and tell you what it is that helps them most in the things that you do; but there is no doubt at all that your recollectedness, your devotional temper, will be one of the things that do help them most. For very many of them, the time that they spend with you in church is the only opportunity which they have of seeing what prayer is; and it is your great opportunity to show them what it is. It is wonderfully impressive to see a soul that really loves God, and really feels awe and delight, speaking to Him; and therefore learning to do that is, surely, a pastoral act? You remember what Penn said of George Fox: 'The most awful, living, reverent frame I ever felt or beheld, was his in prayer' – a tiny vivid picture of a human soul concentrated upon the supernatural world. If you are to help your people thus, you must obtain in your hours of solitude the material for such a supernaturalization of your outward religious life.

All this means that the integration of the whole life, and not any separation of devotion from action – still less a virtual opposition between them – ought to be the priest's ascetic aim, and that the time which you definitely set apart for devotion is to be regarded as contributing to something more than your own personal support and advancement. It is an essential part of your apostolic work. The gentle penetration of every circumstance of life with supernatural values is the mark of the really persuasive type of religion; and this comes neither from a multiplication of suitable services, nor from the promulgation of Christian political ideas, nor yet from the deliberate cultivation of hearty good fellowship of the clerical kind, excellent though all these things may be. It comes always and only from a very pure, childlike and continuous inner life of prayer.

Psychologists tell us that the health and balance of our mental life depend upon the due proportion in it of introversion and extroversion. Now the life of a clergyman in these days is usually and inevitably extroverted to excess. Your attention is incessantly called outwards towards the multitude of details and demands; the clubs and scouts and guides, the weekly social, the monthly magazine, and the whole network of parochial administration. And the result of this, unless you are very careful, is a lack of depth, a spiritual impoverishment, and with it an insidious tendency to attribute undue importance to external details, whether of cultus or of organization; to substitute social and institutional religion for devotional religion. This tendency is now at work right through the ranks of organized Christianity; and, by depriving that organized Christianity of its due supply of supernatural energy, inevitably reduces its redemptive effect. The remedy is to make the private religious life of all such over-busy persons aim at more introversion; and so get the psychic balance right. Their prayer should be of a meditative and recollective type, thus enabling them to give depth and inwardness to their institutional exercises: and – as their inner life matures – helping them to develop that priceless art of prompt recollection at odd times which is unequalled in its power of restoring and stabilizing our adherence to God. Such a scheme need not and should not mean any feverishly intense form of piety. But it does mean such a wise feeding of your souls as will enable you to meet all the demands made upon you without dangerous spiritual exhaustion.

St Bonaventura, in a celebrated passage, divides people of prayer into three main types: first, those who attend chiefly to supplication; next, those who attend chiefly to speculation; and last, those who rise beyond both these to ecstatic communion with God. The classification is obviously based on the threefold promise of Christ, in respect of the prayer that asks, the prayer that seeks and the prayer that knocks at the door: and, like that promise, it exhibits under symbols a profound psychological and spiritual truth – namely the power and range of the soul's effective desire. It is the opinion of Bonaventura that all three types – the intercessor, the theologian, and the contemplative – taken together, are needed to form the Church's life of prayer. I think it is true to say, in a smaller degree, that something of each of these elements is needed too in every complete spiritual life: giving as they do a supernatural objective to the will, the intellect and the heart. Some effective desire and petition, some intellectual seeking, some non-utilitarian, adoring love, are asked of every one of us; and especially of priests. The proportion of each will vary between soul and soul; but it is surely good, in forming our own devotional rule, to keep this complete conception in our minds.

So much, then, for the general aim. What about the means by which we shall secure it? It seems to me that there are four main things which must have a place in any full and healthy religious life: and that a remembrance of this will help us to make our own inner lives balanced and sane. We require, first, the means of gaining and holding a right attitude; secondly, right spiritual food – real, nourishing food with a bite in it, not desiccated and predigested piety. 'I am the food of the full grown,' said the voice of God to St Augustine; 'grow and feed on *Me*.' Thirdly, we need an education which will help growth; training our spiritual powers to an ever greater expansion and efficiency. Fourthly, we have or ought to have some definite spiritual work, and must see that we fit ourselves to do it.

Now each of these four needs is met by a different type of prayer. The right attitude of the soul to God is secured and supported by the prayer of pure adoration. The necessary food for its growth is obtained through our spiritual reading and meditation, as well as by more direct forms of communion. Such meditation will also form an important stage in the education of the spiritual faculties; which are further trained in some degree by the use of such formal, affective or recollective prayer as each one of us is able to employ. Finally, the work which can be done by the praying soul covers the whole field of intercession and redemptive self-oblation.

Take first then, as primary, the achievement and maintenance of a right attitude towards God; that profound and awe-struck sense of His transcendent reality, that humbly adoring relation, on which all else depends. I feel no doubt that, for all who take the spiritual life seriously – and above all for the minister of religion – this prayer of adoration exceeds all other types in educative and purifying power. It alone is able to consolidate our sense of the supernatural, to conquer our persistent self-occupation, to expand our spirits, to feed and quicken our awareness of the wonder and the delightfulness of God. There are two movements which must be plainly present in every complete spiritual life. The energy of its prayer must be directed on the one hand towards God; and on the other towards people. The first movement embraces the whole range of spiritual communion between the soul and God: in it we turn towards Divine Reality in adoration, bathing, so to speak, our souls in the Eternal Light. In the second we return, with the added peace and energy thus gained, to the natural world; there to do spiritual work for and with God for other men. Thus prayer, like the whole of man's inner life, 'swings between the unseen and the seen'. Now both these movements are of course necessary in all Christians, but the point is that the second will only be well done where the first has the central place. The deepening of the soul's unseen attachments must precede, in order that it may safeguard the outward swing towards the world.

This means that adoration, and not intercession or petition, must be the very heart of the life of prayer. For prayer is a supernatural activity or nothing at all; and it must primarily be directed to supernatural ends. It too acknowledges the soul's basic law: it comes from God, belongs to God, is destined for God. It must begin, end, and be enclosed in the atmosphere of adoration; aiming at God for and in Himself. Our ultimate effect as transmitters of the supernal light and love directly depends on this adoring attentiveness. In such a prayer of adoring attentiveness, we open our doors wide to receive His ever-present Spirit; abasing ourselves and acknowledging our own nothingness. Only the soul that has thus given itself to God becomes part of the mystical body through which He acts on life. Its destiny is to be the receiver and transmitter of grace.

Is not that practical work? For Christians, surely, the only practical work. But sometimes we are in such a hurry to transmit that we forget our primary duty is to receive: and that God's self-imparting through us will be in direct proportion to our adoring love and humble receptiveness. Only when our souls are filled to the brim can we presume to offer spiritual gifts to other people. The remedy for that sense of impotence, that desperate spiritual exhaustion which religious workers too often know, is, I am sure, an inner life governed not by petition but by adoring prayer. When we find that the demands made upon us are seriously threatening our inward poise, when we feel symptoms of starvation and stress, we can be quite sure that it is time to call a halt; to re-establish the fundamental relation of our souls with Eternal Reality, the Home and Father of our spirits. 'Our hearts shall have *no* rest save in Thee.' It is only when our hearts are thus actually at rest in God, in peaceful and self-oblivious adoration, that we can hope to show His attractiveness to other people.

In the flood-tide of such adoring prayer, the soul is released from the strife and confusions of temporal life; it is lifted far beyond all petty controversies, petty worries and petty vanities – and none of us escape these things. It is carried into God, hidden in Him. This is the only way in which it can achieve that utter self-forgetfulness which is the basis of its peace and power; and which can never be ours as long as we make our prayer primarily a means of drawing gifts to ourselves and others from God, instead of an act of unmeasured self-giving. I am certain that we gradually and imperceptibly learn more about God by this persistent attitude of humble adoration, than we can hope to do by any amount of mental exploration. For in it our soul recaptures, if only for a moment, the fundamental relation of the tiny created spirit with its Eternal Source, and the time is well spent which is spent in getting this relation and keeping it right. In it we breathe deeply the atmosphere of Eternity; and when we do that, humility and commonsense are found to be the same thing. We realize, and re-realize, our tininess, our nothingness, and the greatness and steadfastness of God. And we all know how priceless such a realization is, for those who have to face the grave spiritual risk of presuming to teach others about Him.

Moreover, from this adoring prayer and the joyous self-immolation that goes with it, all the other prayerful dispositions of our souls seem, ultimately to spring. A deep, humble contrition, a sense of our creaturely imperfection and unworthiness, gratitude for all that is given us, burning and increasing charity that longs to spend itself on other souls – all these things are signs of spiritual vitality: and spiritual vitality depends on the loving adherence of our spirits to God. Thus it is surely of the first importance for those who are called to exacting lives of service, to determine that nothing shall interfere with the development and steady daily practice of loving and adoring prayer; a prayer full of intimacy and awe. It alone maintains the soul's energy and peace, and checks the temptation to leave God for His service. I think that if you have only as little as half an hour to give each morning to your private prayer, it is not too much to make up your minds to spend half that time in such adoration. For it is the central service asked by God of human souls; and its neglect is responsible for much lack of spiritual depth and power. Moreover, it is more deeply refreshing, pacifying and assuring than any other type of prayer. 'Unlike, much unlike,' says à Kempis, 'is the savour of the creator and the creature, of everlastingness and of time, of light uncreate and light illuminate.' But only those know this who are practised in adoring love.

You may reasonably say: This is all very well, and on general religious grounds we shall all agree about the beauty and desirability of such prayer. But how shall we train ourselves, so persistently called away and distracted by a multitude of external duties, to that steadfastly theocentric attitude? This brings us to the consideration of the further elements necessary to the full maintenance of the devotional life – its food and its education. If we want to develop this power of communion, to correspond with the grace that invites us to it, we must nourish our souls carefully and regularly with such noble thoughts of God as we are able to assimilate; and must train our fluctuating attention and feeling to be obedient to the demands of the dedicated will. We must become, and keep, spiritually fit.

We shall, of course, tend to do this feeding and this training in many different ways. No one soul can hope to assimilate all that is offered to us by the richness of Reality. Thus some temperaments are most deeply drawn to adoration by a quiet dwelling upon the spaceless and changeless Presence of God; some, by looking at Christ, or by meditating in a simple way on His acts and words, as recorded in the Gospels, lose themselves in loving communion with Him. Some learn adoration best through the sacramental life. We cannot all feel all these things in their fullness; our spiritual span is not wide enough for that. Therefore we ought to practise humbly and with simplicity those forms of reflective meditation and mental prayer that help us most; and to which, in times of tranquillity, we find ourselves most steadily drawn. We grow by feeding, not by forcing; and should be content in the main to nourish ourselves on the food that we can digest and quietly leave the other kinds for those to whom they appeal. In doing this, however, we shall be wise if we do not wholly neglect even those types of spirituality which attract us least. Thus the natural prayer of the philosophic soul, strongly drawn by the concept of Eternal and Infinite Spirit, becomes too thin, abstract and inhuman if it fails to balance this by some dwelling on the historic and revealed, some sacramental integration of spirit and of sense; the born contemplative drifts into quietism without the discipline of vocal or liturgic prayer; while Christocentric devotion loses depth and awe unless the object of its worship is seen within the horizon of Eternity. Therefore it is well to keep in mind some sense of the rich totality out of which our little souls are being fed.

There is, however, one kind of prayer which all these differing types and levels of spirituality can use and make their own: and which is unequalled in psychological and religious effectiveness. This is the so-called 'prayer of aspirations': the frequent and attentive use of little phrases of love and worship, which help us, as it were, to keep our minds pointing the right way, and never lose their power of forming and maintaining in us an adoring temper of soul. The Psalms, the Confessions of St Augustine, the Imitation of Christ, are full of such aspiratory prayers; which range from the most personal to the most impersonal conceptions of God, and are fitted to every mood and need. They stretch and re-stretch our spiritual muscles; and, even in the stuffiest surroundings, can make us take deep breaths of mountain air. The habit of aspiration is difficult to form, but once acquired exerts a growing influence over the soul's life. Think of St Francis of Assisi repeating all night: 'My God and All! What art Thou? And what am I?' Is not that a perfect prayer of adoration? The humble cry of the awed and delighted creature, gazing at its Creator and Lord. Think of the exclamation of the Psalmist: 'Whom have I in heaven but Thee? And what is there on earth that I desire beside Thee?' Do not all the tangles and tiresome details fall away and vanish when we dwell on such words? And do they not bring us back to the truth, that the most important thing in prayer is never what we say or ask for, but our *attitude* towards God? What it all comes to is this: that the personal religion of the priest must be theocentric. It must conform to the rule laid down by the great Bérulle: that one's true relation to God consists solely in adoration and adherence and that these two moods or attitudes of soul cover the whole range of one's inner life and must be evoked and expressed by prayer.

The question of the proper feeding of our own devotional life must, of course, include the rightful use of spiritual reading. And with spiritual reading we may include formal or informal meditation upon Scripture or religious truth: the brooding consideration, the savouring – as it were the chewing of the cud – in which we digest that which we have absorbed, and apply it to our own needs. Spiritual reading is, or at least it can be, second only to prayer as a developer and support of the inner life. In it we have access to all the hoarded supernatural treasure of the race: all that it has found out about God. It should not be confined to Scripture, but should also include at least the lives and the writings of the canonized and uncanonized saints: for in religion variety of nourishment is far better than a dyspeptic or fastidious monotony of diet. If we do it properly, such reading is a truly social act. It gives to us not only information, but communion; real intercourse with the great souls of the past, who are the pride and glory of the Christian family. Studying their lives and work slowly and with sympathy; reading the family history, the family letters; trying to grasp the family point of view, we gradually discover these people to be in origin though not in achievement very much like ourselves.

They are people who are devoted to the same service, handicapped often by the very same difficulties; and yet whose victories and insights humble and convict us, and who can tell us more and more, as we learn to love more and more, of the relation of the soul to Reality. The Confessions of St Augustine, the Dialogue of St Catherine of Siena, Tauler's Sermons, Gerlac Petersen's 'Fiery Soliloquy with God', the Revelations of Julian of Norwich, the Life of St Teresa, the little book of Brother Lawrence, the Journals of Fox, Woolman and Wesley – the meditative, gentle, receptive reading of this sort of literature immensely enlarges our social and spiritual environment. It is one of the ways in which the communion of saints can be most directly felt by us.

We all know what a help it is to live among, and be intimate with, keen Christians; how much we owe in our own lives to contact with them, and how hard it is to struggle on alone in a preponderantly non-Christian atmosphere. In the saints we always have the bracing society of keen Christians. We are always in touch with the classic standard. Their personal influence still radiates, centuries after they have left the earth, reminding us of the infinite variety of ways in which the Spirit of God acts on people through people, and reminding us too of our own awful personal responsibility in this matter. The saints are the great experimental Christians, who, because of their unreserved self-dedication, have made the great discoveries about God; and, as we read their lives and works, they will impart to us just so much of these discoveries as we are able to bear. Indeed, as we grow more and more, the saints tell us more and more: disclosing at each fresh reading secrets that we did not suspect. Their books are the work of specialists, from whom we can humbly learn more of God and of our own souls.

So the books in constant use in the priests' devotional library might include some at least among those which I have just mentioned; unequalled in their power of widening horizons, taking us away from the spiritual potato-fields in which many of us have to labour, and reminding us of the mountains and the sea. And beyond these, our reading should also extend to those expert manuals of spiritual direction in which is condensed the whole experience of deep and saintly souls – such books as the Imitation of Christ, Augustine Baker's 'Holy Wisdom', that wonderful old pilot-book of the interior life, or Grou's 'Hidden Life of the Soul'. These books are never finished and done with. They are to be read and re-read, incorporated into the very texture of our minds; thus building up a rich and vital sense of all that is involved in the Christian spiritual life

– the deep entrance into reality which it makes possible to ordinary men and women.

Such reading, if properly done, is really a form of prayer. Not only does it give spiritual culture and information, but, what is far more important, it also induces contrition. As we dwell more and more on the spiritual perfection and heroism which is demanded by Christianity, and so quietly and meekly achieved by the great creative servants of God, so does our sense of our own imperfection inevitably deepen. Perhaps the best approach to meditation on one of the great positive Christian virtues – charity, patience, humility – is first to see that virtue in heroic action in the life of one of the saints. And it is always good to meditate on these qualities, because of that law of mental life by which we tend to become that which we behold. We grow best, in fact, not by direct and anxious conflict with our difficulties and bad qualities, but by turning to and gazing at the love, joy and peace of the saints; accepting their standard; setting our wills and desires that way. This is one of the directions in which reading of the type that I have been suggesting can be used to pave the way to the meditation or mental prayer in which we make its lessons our own.

Now meditation not only feeds, it also disciplines the mind and soul; gradually training us to steady our attention upon spiritual things, an art especially difficult to those beset by many responsibilities and duties. It helps us to conquer distractions, and forms with most of us an essential prelude to that state of profound recollection in which the soul dwells almost without effort on the things of God. It is generally and rightly regarded as one of the principal elements in an ordered devotional life. Most people, I suppose, who have taken the trouble to learn it, get their spiritual food very largely by this deliberate exercise of brooding, loving thought; entering into, dwelling on, exploring and personally applying the deeds and the words of Christ or of the saints, or the fundamental conceptions of religion. It is needless to speak here of the various methods by which it can be learnt and practised: they are well known and often described. They resemble each other in training to spiritual ends our chief mental qualities; requiring and teaching the use of visual imagination, feeling, thought and will.

There are people, however, who find that they simply cannot practise these formal and discursive meditations: the effort to do so merely stultifies itself. Where this inability is genuine, and not a disguised laziness, it generally coexists with a strong attraction to a more simple and formless communion with God; that loving and generalized attention which is sometimes called 'simple regard' or 'affective prayer', and has been beautifully described as 'the prayer which articulates nothing but expresses everything: specifies nothing and includes everything'. I think those in whom this tendency is marked and persistent should yield to it, abandon their own efforts and move with docility towards that form of communion to which they feel drawn: remembering that anything we may achieve in the world of prayer only represents our particular way of actualizing one tiny fragment of the supernatural possibilities offered to the race, and that any attempt to reduce the soul's intercourse with the Transcendent to a single system or formula is condemned in advance.

The obstinate pursuit of a special state of meditation or recollection always defeats itself: bringing into operation the law of reversed effort, and concentrating attention on the struggle to meditate instead of on its supernatural end. Yet it is not uncommon to find people forcing themselves from a mistaken sense of duty to develop or continue a devotional method which was never appropriate to their nature, or which they have now outgrown. They deliberately thwart a genuine though as yet unformed attraction to silent communion by struggling hard to perform a daily formal meditation, because they have made this a part of their rule of life; or desperately get through a routine of intercessions and vocal prayers to which they have been injudiciously bound, and which now limit the freedom of their access to God. On the other hand, persons whose natural expression is verbal, and who need the support of concrete image, make violent efforts to 'go into the silence' because some wretched little book has told them to do so. True silent prayer is full of power and beauty; but I suppose few things are more stultifying in effect than this deliberate and artificial passivity. It is not by such devices that we feed the soul; their only result must be spiritual indigestion. Once more, everyone is not nourished by the same sort of food, or invited by God to the same kind of spiritual activity: the rightful variety of Nature is paralleled in the supernatural life. The important thing is to discover what nourishes *you*, best expands and harmonizes *your* spirit, now, at the present stage of your growth.

We have thought a little about the way in which we can use our times of private devotion to confirm us in a right attitude, to nourish our souls; to enlarge our horizons, and deepen our sense of the richness and mystery of God. Now what about our education in prayer? This is a need which presses intimately on each one of us, and from which we are never completely liberated in this life. Here we come to that debatable region where religion and psychology meet. We have to use for our spiritual lives and our spiritual contacts a mental machinery that has been evolved for dealing with the problems and necessities of our bodily lives, and for setting up contacts with the physical world. And that mental machinery, as we all know, is often rebellious and hard to adjust. It is on much more intimate terms with our sensory and motor reactions than it is with our spiritual desires and beliefs. It has a tendency, produced by long habit, to respond easily to every stimulus from the outside world. It has an inherent difficulty in gathering itself together and remaining attentive to the internal world – in technical language, in being recollected. We all have to teach it and persuade it to do that: and even so, this side of its training is never completely achieved. I need not go on about this; it is a fact which every practising Christian knows too well. One great function of regular prayer consists in this training of our mental machinery for the duties asked of it in the devotional life.

It is one of the most distressing aspects of personal religion that we all waste so much of the very limited time which we are able to give to it. The waste can be classified under two main heads: distraction and dryness. No one escapes these, but it concerns us all to reduce them as much as we can. Of dryness I will speak later. As to distraction, this is of two kinds, which we might call fundamental and mechanical. Fundamental distraction is really lack of attention; and lack of attention is really lack of interest. We are seldom distracted where we are truly keen – where the treasure is, the heart is sure to be. St Teresa's advice to her nuns, to 'get themselves some company when first they go to prayer', is one prescription for the cure of fundamental distractedness. Another, particularly suitable for those who find it impossible to forget the pressure of external cares and legitimate interests, consists in making those very cares and interests the subject-matter of the prayer, thus conquering the distraction by absorption instead of by conflict. Mechanical distraction, on the other hand, seems to be connected with the element of reverie which is present in meditation and mental prayer; and the difficulty, inherent in this type of thinking, of maintaining complete concentration. In such mechanical distraction the deeper soul remains steadfast in prayer, the will and intention do not vary; but recollection is disturbed by involuntary thoughts and images which perpetually pass across the field of consciousness. The remedy for this is a steady, patient training of the mind; the gradual formation of channels along which our devotional energies can flow.

Vocal prayer, rightly used, is particularly valuable here. Vocal prayers, as we know, give no information to

God: but they do give to us that temper of mind in which we can approach Him. They are the ways in which we tune our receiver in. If anyone objects that this is tantamount to saying that vocal prayer is a self-suggestion, I reply that a very great deal of it *is* self-suggestion; and moreover that we ought thus to suggest to our reluctant and wandering minds such devotional ideas. It is a method which has been given to us by God. It has always been used by religious persons; and we ought not to be afraid of doing that which has always been done with profit, merely because psychology has given to it a new and ugly name. Formal prayer is a practical device, not a spiritual necessity. It makes direct suggestions to our souls; reminding us of realities which we always tend to forget. It harnesses attention to the matter in hand; captures our psychic machinery, and directs it to a spiritual end. This is not merely the impious opinion of psychology. It is also that of the great masters of prayer. 'It is not necessary,' says Grou, 'in order that we may be heard of God, that we should have recourse to formal acts, even those of a purely interior kind: and if we produce these in our prayer, it is less for Him than for ourselves, in order to maintain our attention in His presence. Our weakness often demands the help of such acts – but they are not of the essence of prayer.'

If this principle were grasped, the supposed unreal and mechanical character of regular vocal prayer, which worries some people, would cease to trouble us. Properly used, it can gradually train us to a continuous sense of the Presence of God. Especially valuable for this purpose is that practice of aspirations, or short acts, to which I have already referred. Many of these 'acts', when we dwell on their meaning, are jewels of devotion, wonderful in their claim and demand, and capable of opening up to us the great world of contemplation. They give the mind something to hold on to; quiet it, and persuade us to feel the love, penitence or joy which they suggest. They lull distracting thoughts and gradually train our mental life to run, more and more, in the channels they mark out. Such habits when formed – and the formation does take time – are for the busy worker an immense source of security and peace.

I would go further than this, and say that what is known as the James-Lange law has a direct bearing on the devotional life. That is to say, that our emotions are very closely connected with, and often even evoked by, the appropriate gestures and muscular movements which have become associated with them. Thus, for instance, kneeling does tend to put us in a prayerful mood, and many other more elaborate ritual actions, which persons of common sense too easily dismiss, are psychologically justified on the same count. That instinctive psychologist, St Ignatius, who leaves nothing to chance, gives very careful and exact directions for the bodily behaviour of those who are going through the Spiritual Exercises. Before beginning a meditation, for instance, he recommends retreatants to stand still, a few paces from the spot where the meditation is to be made, and there to recollect themselves; raising their minds to God, and considering Christ as present and attentive to that which they are about to do. Only after this pause, which is to be long enough for the recital of the Lord's Prayer, may the retreatants advance, and 'take up the attitude most suitable to the end proposed'. This may all sound very artificial; but I think that anyone who gives it a trial for a week will have to acknowledge at the end that St Ignatius knew a good deal about how to control the human mind. We shall never become spiritual until we acknowledge the humbling fact that we are half animal still, and must suit our practices to our condition.

Finally I want to say something about a factor which is always present in every developed life of prayer: the liability to spiritual dryness and blankness, painful to all fervent Christians, but specially distressing to those whose business it is to work with souls. The times when all your interest and sense of reality evaporate; when the language of religion becomes meaningless and you are quite unable, in any real sense, to pray. Everyone is so off-colour from time to time; and it is one of the great problems of the priest and religious teacher, to know how, under these conditions, he can best serve God and other souls. Now first of all, it is possible to reduce the intensity of such desolations – to use the technical term – by wise handling of yourselves; and here prudent self-treatment is plainly your duty – the dictates of grace and common sense coincide. The condition is largely psychological. It is a fatigue state; a reaction sometimes from excessive devotional fervour, sometimes from exacting spiritual work, which has exhausted the inner reserves of the soul. It almost always follows on any period of marked spiritual progress or enlightenment. In either case, the first point is, accept the situation quietly. Don't aggravate it, don't worry, don't dwell on it, don't have contrition about it; but turn, so far as you can, to some secular interest or recreation and *'wait* till the clouds roll by'. Many a priest ends every Sunday in the state of exhaustion in which he cannot possibly say his own prayers; in which, as one of them observed, the only gift of the Spirit in which he is able to take any interest is a hot bath. That is a toll levied by his psychophysical limitations. Effort and resistance will only make it worse.

But it is a toll that can be turned into a sacrifice. It is one of the most painful obligations of the life of the religious worker, that he is often called upon to help other souls when he is in desolation himself. He has got to put a good face on it – to listen to their raptures or their despairs – to give himself without stint in serving – never to betray anything of his own inner state. And this is one of the most purifying of all experiences that can come to him; for it contains absolutely no food for self-satisfaction, but throws him completely back upon God. I think it is above all in work done in times of aridity and desolation that the devotional life of the priest shows its worth.

Part III

❂

CONTEMPLATION AND
CREATIVE WORK

THE SAYING OF ST IGNATIUS WHICH WE TOOK AS A TEXT when considering the essential character of the inner life, declared that 'man was created to praise, reverence and serve the Lord his God'. Not to try to be something which he or she is not, or strain after that which is inaccessible: but here and now, with the means provided, completely to fulfil this destiny of humanity.

If we have indeed begun to do this, if the praise and the reverence of God, the awed delight in His realness, do indeed dominate our inner life, and are conditioning the development in us of a spiritual personality; then surely the result must issue in some form of spiritual service. Because human beings are partly spirit, and already possess something of the creative character of spirit, their delight and awe must be expressed in work; spiritual work accomplished by spiritual means. As their supernatural lives expand, so must their supernatural effectiveness increase. This brings us to the last of the four implicits of a healthy life of prayer. It must maintain the human soul in adoration, must nourish it, and educate its faculties, and must produce creative work.

The first obvious meaning which religious persons instinctively attach to spiritual work is, of course, intercession. But spiritual work can – and surely, especially in priests, it should – cover a much wider range than intercession as we commonly conceive of it. We said that the healthy expansion of the spiritual life depends on the balance struck between two movements; the direction of the soul's love and energy first towards God and then towards other people. We have dwelt especially on the character of its initial movement towards God; the total surrender and confidence which are demanded of it, and then the feeding, deepening and stabilizing of that communion and the education of the soul for and in it – in fact the nature and the nurture of a person's supernatural life. What is the ultimate object of all this process? Surely not mere spiritual self-cultivation; a horrible idea for any soul, but especially for a minister of religion. The object can only be to make the soul more creative, more effective, more useful to God: to increase in it spiritual energy, genuine and fruitful personality. To make it, in fact, more and more capable of work: all those devoted activities, not merely of body and mind but also of the spirit, which are demanded of a shepherd of a spiritual flock. You remember how St Teresa, one of the greatest of contemplatives, insisted that the one real object of the spiritual marriage – a term which means, on her lips, not an emotional rapture but the completely transfiguring and creative union of the soul with God – was simply the production of *work*.

There is a wonderful chapter in Ruysbroeck's 'Book of the Twelve Béguines' in which he describes the life of one who has achieved this state, as 'ministering to the world without in love and in mercy; whilst inwardly abiding in simplicity, in stillness, and in utter peace'. Reading it, we remember that it was said of Ruysbroeck himself, that supreme mystic, that during the years in which he was a parish priest in Brussels, he went to and fro in the streets of the city 'with his mind perpetually lifted up into God'. He was ministering to the world without in love and mercy; whilst inwardly abiding in simplicity, stillness, and utter peace. Action, effort and tension, then, are to be the outward expression and substance of such a life of spiritual creativeness; yet all this is to hang on and be nurtured by an inward abidingness in simplicity, stillness and peace. We are called upon to carry the Eternal and Unchanging right through every detail of our changeful active life, because and by means of our daily secret recourse to and concentration upon it. Is it not in practising this lovely and costly art, gradually getting at home with it, that we more and more transmute and deify the very substance even of our temporal life? Thus more and more we are doing the special work of the human soul, as a link between the worlds of spirit and of sense.

If we elect for such a career, join up thus with the Divine activities of the universe, almost at once we begin to find that the supernatural energy acts not only on us but through us. Our contact with other people is changed. Our spirit touches and modifies theirs, often unconsciously. We find ourselves more and more able to use, expand and share the supernatural power received in our own prayer; and this for the most part in very simple and unpremeditated ways. This power will show itself in *you*, in your quickened sense of the needs and character of the souls that have been put into your charge; and in the conflict with evil, not merely in its expression but at its very source, to which also you are committed. All this concerns you in your vocation as priests very specially; and all this you will inevitably long to do more and more, as the life of adoration deepens in your soul. The effect of that life is bound to be the awakening of an ever more wide-spreading, energetic, self-giving and redeeming type of love.

Now intercession is such a love as that, acting and serving in the atmosphere of prayer; and in it we do actually reach out to, penetrate and affect other souls. That we should do this, seems to be implicit in the mysterious economy of the spiritual life. It is a feeble imitation on the part of our small, derivative and growing spirits of the way in which the Holy Spirit of God reaches out to and acts on us; moulding and guiding us, both secretly within the soul and outwardly by means of persons and events. When we think of what the greatest spiritual personality we have ever known did for us, in harmonizing us and compelling us to feel reality, and if we multiply this to the nth degree, it gives us a hint of the intensity and subtlety of the workings of the eternal and living Spirit in and through people on other people; and the volume of supernatural work which is waiting for us, when we have sufficient love, courage and humility to do it.

Such a view of the obligation laid upon us, centres on the fundamental religious truth of the Divine prevenience: of the Supernatural, of God, seeking men and women through natural means, and disclosed to them, above all, through personality. It is hence, above all, in trying to work thus for and with God that the soul grows, and as the soul grows, so more and more it craves to do such work. The command to Peter, 'Feed my sheep', was just as good for Peter as it was for the sheep. The saints are our great exemplars of this dual life of adoration and intercession; that complete and balanced Christianity involving the extreme of industrious and disinterested love, which seeks to spread and incarnate in the time-world the changeless Spirit of Eternity.

Put in that way, spiritual work sounds very transcendental, and seems to demand a degree of power and of sanctity beyond the common Christian range. But St Teresa, with her marked instinct for coming down to brass tacks, pointed out that the guarantee of that union with God in which alone such work can be done, was not to be found in any lofty or abnormal type of experience. It was to be found, above all, in the combination of an ever deepening personal lowliness, an ever more vivid love of our neighbour, and an ever keener sense of the holy character of daily work – getting, so to speak, Divine perfection into our little daily jobs. These three qualities involve, first, that sense of our creaturely status, that meek, childlike dependence which is the only source of peace; next the perfect and equal charity which is the sweetener of every relation of life, and 'loves the unlovely into loveableness'; last, that unlimited devotedness, that unfastidious joy in service perfectly achieved, which transforms the whole daily routine, religious and secular, into a spiritual activity.

They require of us that quiet doing of our job, in sun and in fog, which distinguishes generosity from emotion, and gives backbone to the dedicated life. Her test means that until the life of prayer flowers in this perfect integration of the outward and the inward, it is not functioning rightly, and we are not doing the full work to which the human soul is called – we are stopping half-way.

This can only mean that the first concern of a fully Christian life is with the realm of Being; with God Himself, to whom each one in our ceaseless series of outward acts and experiences must be related. And its second concern is with the bringing of the values of that world of Being into the world of Becoming, the physical world of succession and change. That, of course, is putting the situation in a roughly philosophic way. We put it in a more religious way if we say that such a scheme of life commits us to carrying on in our own small measure the dual redemptive and illuminating work of Christ; and this by such a willing and unlimited surrender, such love, humility and diligence, as shall make us agents of the Eternal within the world of time. All this means once more, that when in our own practice we really develop a creative inner life, we are sure to find that it involves us in a twofold activity; an activity directed both to God and to other souls.

Thus the complete life of the Christian worker is and must be, in more than a metaphorical sense, a continuous life of prayer. It requires a constant inward abiding in God's atmosphere; an unhesitating response to His successive impulsions; a steady approximation to more and more perfect union with His creative will. We can test the increase of our souls in depth, strength and reality, by the improvement in our ability to maintain this state. Formal prayers, corporate or solitary, are merely the skeleton of this life and are largely intended to tune us up and educate us for it. It has, of course, always been the Christian view, that every bit of work done towards God *can* be a prayer: and every action of life directly related to Him. The holy woman who was accustomed to boil her potatoes for the intentions of those people for whom she had not time to pray, was merely putting this principle into practice. Such a direction of desire in and through the sensible to the very heart of the supra-sensible is close to the central secret of the sacramental life. But this perfect harmony of inward and outward is the privilege of spiritual maturity and no one will achieve it who does not make a definite place each day for the feeding and deepening of direct communion, the stretching and strengthening of the soul. How then are *you*, in your special circumstances, going to weave together prayer and outward action into the single perfect fabric of the apostolic life? I just mention three among the many ways in which it seems to me that the clergy can do this: making their inner life of prayer continuously and directly useful to those to whom they are sent, incorporating it with their pastoral activities.

I put first a very simple thing; a thing which I imagine that almost everyone can do, and which I have never known to fail in its effect. It is this. Make time to pray in your own churches as much as you possibly can. That is the first move towards making these churches real houses, schools and homes of prayer, which very often they are not. I do not mean by this merely saying Matins and Evensong in them. I mean, let at least part of the time which is given to your real and informal communion with God be spent in your own church. That is the best and most certain way in which to give our churches the atmosphere of devotion which we all recognize so quickly when we find it, and which turns them into spiritual homes; and I believe it is one of the most valuable forms of Christian witness which can be exercised by the clergy in the present day.

It seems to me that it is very little use to keep a church open, unless its own priest does care to go into it and pray in it. You might just as well, in most cases, keep a waiting-room open. Surely it is part of your business to make your church homely and lovable, and especially, if you can, to give it a welcoming aspect at those hours when the working people who so greatly need its tranquillizing atmosphere can inconspicuously slip in. It is useless to talk at large to those working people, mostly living without privacy in noisy streets, about the reality and necessity of prayer unless you provide a quiet place in which they can practise it. It must be a place which does not receive them with that forbidding air of a spiritual drawing-room in dust-sheets, peculiar to many Anglican churches during the week; but which abounds in suitable suggestions, offers an invitation which it helps them to accept. A place, in fact, to which your own prayers have helped to give the requisite quality of homeliness. This creation of a real supernatural home, and steady practice of a real supernatural hospitality, is the first point, it seems to me, in which a clergyman can hardly fail to make his inner life directly serve his flock.

The next direction in which it is possible for you to make your self-training in prayer useful to those in your charge falls under the general head of intercession. That will, of course, include all that you can do for your parish and for individuals in the way of support, in the way of tranquillizing and healing influences, in the way of supernatural guidance by the loving meditations and prayers which you spend upon them. Those who deal much with souls soon come to know something about the strange spiritual currents which are at work under the surface of life, and the extent to which charity can work on supernatural levels for supernatural ends. But if you are to do that, the one thing that matters is that you should care supremely about it; care, in fact, so much that you do not mind how much you suffer for it. We cannot help anyone until we do care, for it is only by love that spirit penetrates spirit.

Consider for a moment what is implied in this amazing mystery of intercession; at least in the little that we understand of it. It implies first our implicit realization of God, the infinitely loving, living and all-penetrating Spirit of Spirits, as an Ocean in which we all are bathed. And next, speaking still that spatial language to which our human thinking is tied down, that somehow through this uniting and vivifying medium we too, being one with Him in love and will, can mutually penetrate, move and influence each other's souls in ways as yet unguessed; yet throughout the whole process moulded and determined by the prevenient, personal, free and ever-present God. The world He has been and is creating is a world infused through and through with Spirit; and it is partly through the prayerful and God-inspired action of men and women that the spiritual work of this world is done. When a man or woman of prayer, through devoted concentration, reaches a soul in temptation and rescues it, we must surely acknowledge that this is the action of God Himself using that person as an instrument.

In this mysterious interaction of energies it seems that one tool is put into our hands: our love, will, interest, desire – four words describing four aspects of one thing. This dynamic love, once purged of self-interest, is ours to use on spiritual levels; it is an engine for working with God on other souls. The saints so used it, often at tremendous cost to themselves, and with tremendous effect. As their personalities grew in strength and expanded in adoration, so they were drawn on to desperate and heroic wrestling for souls; to those exhausting and creative activities, that steady and generous giving of support, that redeeming prayer by which human spirits are called to work with God. Especially in its most mysterious reaches, in its redemptive, self-immolating action on suffering and sin, their intercession dimly reproduces and continues the supernatural work of Christ. Real saints do feel and bear the weight of the sins and pains of the world. It is the human soul's greatest privilege that we can thus accept redemptive suffering for one another – and they do.

'God *enabled* me to agonize in prayer,' said the saintly evangelical, David Brainerd. 'My soul was drawn out very much for the world. I grasped for a multitude of souls.' Does not that give to us a sense of unreached possibilities, of deep mysterious energies; something not quite covered by what are usually called 'intercessions'? So too St Teresa says that if anyone claiming to be united to God is always in a state of peaceful beatitude, she simply does not believe in their union with God. Such a union, to her mind, involves great sorrow for the sin and pain of the world; a sense of identity not only with God but also with all other souls, and a great longing to redeem and heal. That is real supernatural charity. It is a call to love and save not the nice but the nasty; not the lovable but the unlovely, the hard, the narrow, and the embittered, and the tiresome, who are so much worse. To love irrespective of merit or opinion or personal preference; to love even those who offend our taste. If you are to love your people thus, translating your love, as you must, into unremitting intercessory work, and avoid being swamped by the great ocean of suffering, sin and need to which you are sent; once again this will only be done by maintaining and feeding the temper of adoration and trustful adherence. This is the heart of the life of prayer; and only in so far as we work from this centre can we safely dare to touch other souls and seek to affect them. For such intercession is a sacrificial job; and sacrificial jobs need the support of a strong inner life if they are to be carried through. They are rooted and grounded in love.

The third obvious way in which the priest's life of prayer reacts upon his flock, is in the personal advice and guidance which he is able to give to those who consult him to use a technical word, in direction work. What is direction? It is the guidance of one soul by and through another soul. It is the individual and intensive side of pastoral work. God comes to and affects individuals very largely through other individuals; and you, in your ordination, all offered yourselves for this. The relation of discipleship is one that obtains right through and down all stages of the spiritual life; giving to it a definite social structure, protecting it from subjectivism and lawlessness, and ensuring its continuity. Hence all that we may have been given or gained we ought ever to be ready to impart.

Such direction work is surely one of the most sacred of human duties; and as your inner life becomes stronger and your spiritual sensitiveness increases, so more souls will inevitably come to you for it, and more and more of its difficulties and possibilities will be revealed. Therefore a solemn obligation rests on the priest, doesn't it, to train his mind as well as his soul for this work? To learn, for instance, something of the mental peculiarities of man, especially as they affect his religious life; to recognize the various stages and types of spirituality, and find out how best to deal with them; to discern spirits, and to distinguish their different aptitudes and needs. In its fullness such discernment is a special gift; but something of it is surely possible to all of us, if we take enough interest in souls. Direction work can, of course, be done only and all the time in absolute interior dependence on God; and all the most valuable part of it will be done silently, by the influence of your prayer on the souls that you are called upon to guide. You will find it a perfectly possible and practicable thing to reach out to them and mould them in that way; and if they are at all sensitive, they will probably become aware that you are doing it.

Amongst those who are likely to come to the clergy for spiritual advice are three outstanding classes. First, quite young people, including Confirmation candidates, who are at the beginning of their spiritual, mental and emotional lives, and wish for guidance in religion. Secondly, adults who have lost their faith, or have never had it, but who now want to be helped to find God. Thirdly, adults who are still Christian, but who are tortured by doubts, or over-tried by life; and who want to be helped not to lose God. Here the first principle surely is that in each class each person must be envisaged separately; and in each case the directing soul must think first not of its own point of view, not of any set doctrinal scheme, any 'Catholic' or 'evangelical' principles, but of that one inquiring soul in its special needs, its special stage of advancement, its special relation to God.

You are face to face with a living, growing individual spirit; not a lump of wax on which to stamp the Christian seal. And you are responsible to God, not for giving that soul a bit of orthodox information, which it probably won't understand: but for helping it to see its own whereabouts, actualize in its own way its particular spiritual capacities, that it may gradually become more real, and fulfil its latent genius for sanctity. Hence the first temptation which the director must conquer at all costs, is the inclination to generalize, to apply stock ideas. Even with the young and untried, routine instructions and methods are often dangerous; for already, at the very beginning, soul differs immensely from soul. A great respect for every type and size, homely patience, humble self-oblivion, a sense of the slowness of real spiritual growth; these are the qualities which make the good director. The teacher is often inclined to force the pace with the ardent; whereas wise moderation in direction, a gentle willingness to wait, is perhaps the one thing that is always safe with everyone all the time.

With the second and third class of souls it is of course even more imperative to be self-oblivious, slow and tentative; for here you are dealing with more or less developed but troubled minds, alertly awake to the least hint of unreality, suspicious of theological formulas, and probably unwilling to accept without criticism anything that you say. Moreover, you are necessarily only partly acquainted with their mental furnishing and outlook; and therefore it is never possible for you to be certain what exact meaning your words will convey, and what effect they will produce. The emotional aura surrounding religious ideas is of all things most difficult to estimate. Your pet symbols may turn out to be those which are most calculated to put your pupils off. In dealing with such cases, you are or should be perpetually thrown back on God. You can only hope to deal with them at all in a spirit of prayer; and in constant remembrance that the one thing which really matters is the contagious character of your own certitude, never the argument by which it is expressed. So done, the result of your work will often surprise you, and seem to bear little relation to anything that you have been able to say.

Even with those persons who are or seem most impressionable and most sympathetic to you, it is a help to realize from the first that you will never be able to make another soul see reality from exactly the same spiritual angle as yourself. You will not, indeed, be able to transfer even the most fundamental of your convictions to them with no change of colour or meaning. Nor should you wish to do so; for a good deal of that colour and emphasis is your personal contribution, and has little to do with absolute truth. Your pupils inevitably bring to their encounter with God a psychic content which is entirely different from yours; hence, in psychological language, their apperceptive mass will be peculiar to themselves, coloured by their education, tastes, character, past history and social environment. Now apperception controls all our religious insights and experiences; which, so long as we are in the body, cannot by any possibility be pure. The result of this psychological law is that your most careful and precise teaching often fails to find acceptance; or else comes back to you in an unrecognizable form. This, if you attribute absolute value to the particular terms in which you gave it, may be a very disheartening experience, and administer a sound slap to professional self-esteem.

But in proportion as your interior life of prayer grows deep, tender and selfless, in proportion as you value forms only as the clothing of inwardly perceived realities, so will you be able to get away from the conventional phraseology which now puts many people off so terribly, and adapt your language to the particular circumstances of each soul. It is a remarkable note of the Gospels that they make clear to us how many different ways our Lord had of saying the same thing; how He met each type on its own ground, and was satisfied to ask some to find the Father through contemplation of the lilies, whilst of others was demanded self-stripping and the Cross. And it still remains true that the most saintly teachers are always the most varied, winning, unrigoristic and persuasive in their methods; however hard and costly the demands which they may ultimately make.

This means seeing all such work from a really pastoral angle; keeping your eye steadily on the size, sort, appetite and future development of each particular sheep, trying to help each to achieve *their* sort of perfection, not yours, refusing the temptation to 'form a type', and aiming all the time at life, more abundant life for each, and the giving and fostering of it. Not at imparting information, but providing suitable food which can and must be digested; and changed, as real food must be in the process, in order that it may nourish the life of the creature fed. When you see the situation in this way, you cease to mind the fact that those bits which *you* think the very best are often ignored, and your most careful suggestions and instructions are apparently misunderstood. After all, the spiritual personality you are helping to form is probably quite different from your own; and perhaps even different from your own secret ideal for it. Hence the very things that may seem to you most essential or most excellent must not always be pressed. Mangel-wurzels do not suit every sheep at every stage of its growth. It needs a great deal of self-abandonment to do all this with simplicity – it means learning from those who come to you, as well as trying to teach – and that is the purifying part of personal religious work.

Moreover those who do this work are commonly themselves growing and changing; they have not arrived, but are travelling and exploring as they go. It is generally a case of one more or less dusty pilgrim helping another *in via*; not of an established professor, who knows all about it, administering stock teaching to a docile student. It may very well happen that someone will come to you for advice, who has had or seems to have had spiritual experiences far beyond your present range; or who had been called to a form of prayer of which you know nothing at first hand. What is to be done about that? How are you going to distinguish the victims of nervous illness or of religious vanity from those who have a genuine drawing to religion of the mystical type? And how, in this latter case – the case of those drawn by God to the mystical degrees of prayer, often to their own great bewilderment – are you going to give just the help and guidance their souls need, in regions where you yourself have never been? This humbling duty may be laid at any moment on any member of the clergy; and it will be an awful thing, won't it, if you have concentrated so entirely on the parochial, ethical and humanitarian side of religion that you have nothing to give souls that are called to practise its deeper mysteries?

This is where a strict personal training in mental prayer and spiritual reading abundantly justifies itself. You may not yourself be called to the mountains; but you will be more able to advise and understand prospective mountaineers if you have at least put on heavy boots and tried a little hill-climbing, than if you have merely spent all your time on the level, growing nice little patches of devotional mustard and cress. And those who thus form and maintain in themselves the disciplined habit of attention to God, who exercise their spiritual muscles, quicken their spiritual senses, and try to learn their business from the saints, do develop the power of discriminating the self-deluded from the genuine mystical type; by no means an easy thing to do. They recognize the real thing when they meet it; and have access to sources of information which they know how to apply, and which do enable them to help it. There is no doubt at all that human souls can be and are thus used by God, to help other souls more spiritually advanced than themselves; but only if they are in touch through surrendered prayer with the sources of spiritual light. It is useless, indeed dangerous, to read works on mystical prayer and presume to apply them, unless we have to some extent sought to practise the discipline of recollection ourselves. We think that we understand them, and we don't; we try to apply them, and come hopelessly to grief. Spiritual books are written in the language of the spirit; and must be spiritually discerned. They yield a new sense at every reading; and it is only after many years that most of us begin to realize the colossal nature of our own initial mistakes. Hence it is imperative that those called to guide the souls of others, should themselves be humble pupils in the school of interior prayer.

This idea of the call of God to one soul to be the director, support and light-giver to another soul, has rather fallen out of our English religious life. It is at present only practised in one branch of the Church; and there very often in what seems to be an unnecessarily hot-housey way. The detailed and personal work with souls done in past ages by the numerous men and women, both lay and religious, who transmitted the science of the spiritual life, is now forgotten. We are much concerned about various kinds of education, but we leave wholly on one side this parental, patient and expert training and cherishing of the spirit. And yet how beautiful, how Christian, and how natural an idea it is! The work of the great French directors – Fénelon, Bossuet, François de Sales, Vincent de Paul – shows what it can do, and what gentle wisdom, moderation, flexibility, psychological insight, selfless patience and spiritual firmness it demands. Their letters of direction, which ought surely to be read and re-read by every priest, are full of that sanctified common sense which weaves together with a firm hand the worlds of nature and of grace; and helps the pupil soul to find, in all the ordinary circumstances of life, material for prayer and discipline and an opportunity of getting nearer to reality. I think the revival, in a form adapted to our times, of such personal direction work would do much to renew the life of prayer within the English Church; and it cannot be restored without a sufficiency of clergy able to undertake it. Those who are able are not likely to lack pupils very long: they are easily recognized, and the present widespread hunger for the things of the spirit does the rest.

Now let us sum up the substance of what we have been considering. First, the obvious truth that the servant of God cannot do his best unless he is his best: and therefore self-deepening and self-improvement are the very heart of his job. Secondly, that being one's best, for Christians, depends on and requires the active co-operation and close union of God's grace and our will: docility and effort both at once. That this union of serene docility and costly effort, then, must rule in the priest's life of prayer: for the object of that life of prayer is the deepening and expanding of your own inner life, an ever more perfect self-oblation, in order that you may be able to apprehend, receive and pass on to others more and more of the abundant secrets of Eternal Life. Out of *your* struggles and temptations, *your* tentative glimpses of reality, *your* generous acts of utter self-abandonment to the purposes of God – out of all these different kinds of purification taken together, something has to be made, with which the Holy Spirit can do His work on other souls. Because that is the way in which He does do His work on other souls. In other words, our deepest life consists in a willed correspondence with the world of Spirit, and this willed correspondence, which is prayer, is destined to fulfil itself along two main channels; in love towards God and in love towards humanity – two loves which at last and at their highest become one love. Sooner or later, in varying degrees, the power and redeeming energy of God will be manifested through those who thus reach out in desire, first towards Him and then towards other souls. And we, living and growing personalities, are required to become ever more and more spiritualized, ever more and more persuasive, more and more deeply real; in order that we may fulfil this Divine purpose.

This is not mere pious fluff. This is a terribly practical job; the only way in which we can contribute to the bringing in of the Kingdom of God. Humanitarian politics will not do it. Theological restatement will not do it. Holiness *will* do it. And for this growth towards holiness, it seems that it is needful to practise, and practise together, both that genuine peaceful recollection in which the soul tastes, and really knows that the Lord is sweet, inwardly abiding in His stillness and peace; and also the suffering, effort and tension required of us unstable human creatures, if we are to maintain that interior state and use it for the good of other people. This ideal is so rich that in its wholeness it has only been satisfied once. Yet it is so elastic that within it every faithful personality can find a place and opportunity of development. It means the practice of both attachment and detachment; the most careful and loving fulfilment of all our varied this-world obligations, without any slackening of attachment to the other-worldly love. And if we want a theoretical justification of such a scheme of life, surely we have it in the central Christian doctrine of the Incarnation? For does not this mean the Eternal, Changeless God reaching out to win and eternalize His creatures by contact through personality? That the direct action of Divine Love on man is through man; and that God requires our growth in personality, in full being, in order that through us His love and holiness can more and more fully be expressed? And our Lord's life of ministry supported by much lonely prayer gives us the classic pattern of human correspondence with this, our twofold environment. The saints tried to imitate that pattern more and more closely; and as they did so, their personalities expanded and shone with love and power. They show us in history a growth and transformation of character which we are not able to grasp; yet which surely ought to be the Christian norm? In many cases they were such ordinary, even unpromising people when they began; for the real saint is neither a special creation nor a spiritual freak. He is just a human being in whom has been fulfilled the great aspiration of St Augustine – 'My life shall be a real life, being wholly full of Thee.' And as that real life, that interior union with God grows, so too does the saints' self-identification with humanity grow. They do not stand aside wrapped in delightful prayers and feeling pure and agreeable to God. They go right down into the mess; and there, right down in the mess, they are able to radiate God because they possess Him. And that, above all else, is the priestly work that wins and heals souls.'